How the
COMPUTER
CHANGED HISTORY

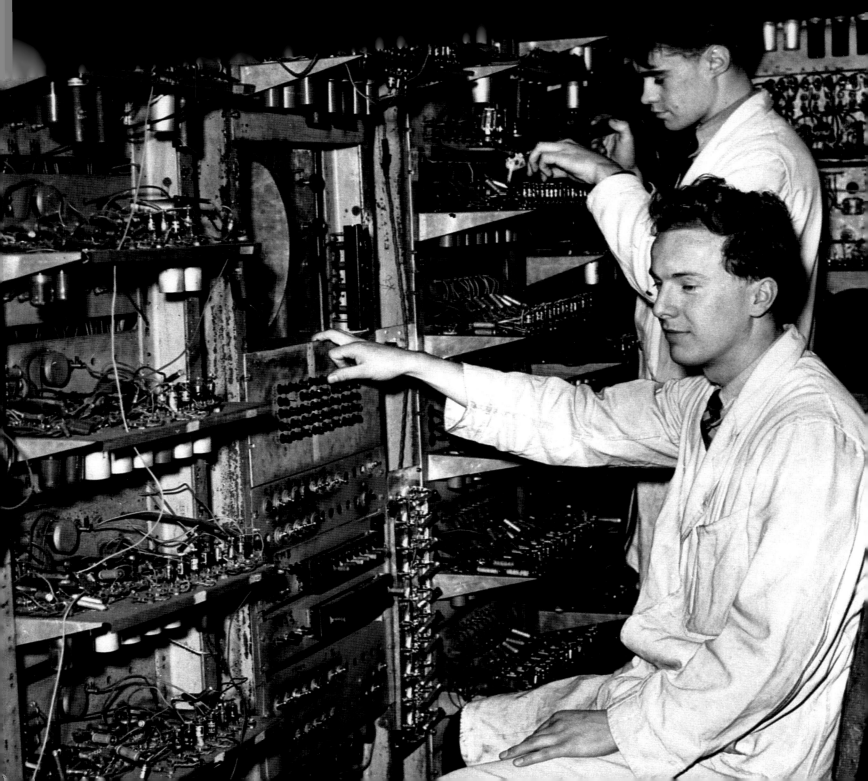

How the
COMPUTER
CHANGED HISTORY

by Therese Naber

CONTENT CONSULTANT

Janet Abbate, PhD

Associate Professor, Science & Technology in Society

Virginia Tech

ESSENTIAL LIBRARY OF
INVENTIONS

Essential Library

An Imprint of Abdo Publishing | abdopublishing.com

abdopublishing.com

Published by Abdo Publishing, a division of ABDO, PO Box 398166, Minneapolis, Minnesota 55439. Copyright © 2016 by Abdo Consulting Group, Inc. International copyrights reserved in all countries. No part of this book may be reproduced in any form without written permission from the publisher. Essential Library™ is a trademark and logo of Abdo Publishing.

Printed in the United States of America, North Mankato, Minnesota
052015
092015

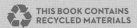

Cover Photo: Stephen Rudolph/Shutterstock Images
Interior Photos: University of Manchester/PA Wire URN:6068959/AP Images, 2, 42; Bettmann/Corbis, 6–7, 23, 31, 33, 36–37, 46–47, 49; Everett Collection/Shutterstock Images, 9, 52; Shutterstock Images, 13, 99 (bottom); Marc Dietrich/Shutterstock Images, 15; AP Images, 16–17, 26–27, 39, 66; iStockphoto, 19, 55 (top right), 55 (middle left), 55 (middle right), 55 (bottom left), 55 (bottom right), 99 (top); Photos.com/Thinkstock, 21; David Duprey/AP Images, 25; Everett Collection/Newscom, 29; Barış Muratoğlu/iStockphoto, 55 (top left); Karsten Lemm/DPA/Corbis, 56–57; RK/AP Images, 59; William Berry/Atlanta Journal-Constitution/AP Images, 61; DB Apple/DPA/Corbis, 63; Josie Lepe/MCT/Newscom, 68; Apple Computer/AP Images, 71; Carmine Galasso/KRT/Newscom, 72–73; Don Fogg/Cooper-Hewitt/National Design Museum/AP Images, 75; Brian Kersey/AP Images, 78; Jochen Tack/ImageBroker/Newscom, 80; Stephen Krow/iStockphoto, 81; Max Herman/Shutterstock Images, 85; Stefano Tinti/Shutterstock Images, 86–87; Paul Sakuma/AP Images, 89; Jon Super/AP Images, 90; Seth Wenig/AP Images, 92–93; Michael Kappeler/Picture-Alliance/DPA/AP Images, 96; Giuseppe Costantino/Shutterstock Images, 98

Editor: Mirella Miller
Series Designer: Craig Hinton

Library of Congress Control Number: 2015930958

Cataloging-in-Publication Data

Naber, Therese.
 How the computer changed history / Therese Naber.
  p. cm. -- (Essential library of inventions)
Includes bibliographical references and index.
ISBN 978-1-62403-782-5
1. Computers--History--Juvenile literature.   2. Inventions--Juvenile literature.
I. Title.
004--dc23

                                         2015930958

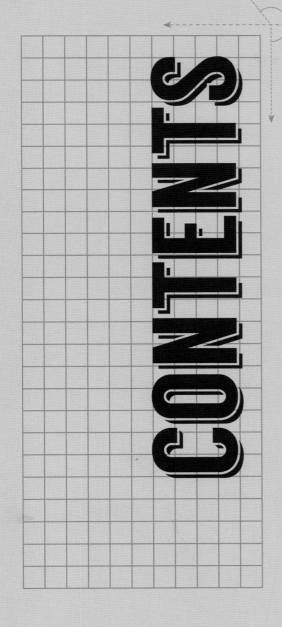

CONTENTS

CHAPTER 1

THE INTERCONNECTIONS
PROBLEM

Computers are everywhere today. But these modern machines have existed for only a few decades. The first electronic digital computers were created in the 1940s for military purposes, and they were costly, room-filling machines. The military needed computers for activities such as breaking enemy code and performing calculations to improve the accuracy of artillery fire. By the 1950s, computers were being mass-produced for business, government, and scientific use, but they were still very large and very expensive. One key technology that helped reduce the size and cost of computers was the transistor, invented in 1947 and used in the wildly popular transistor radio in the mid-1950s.

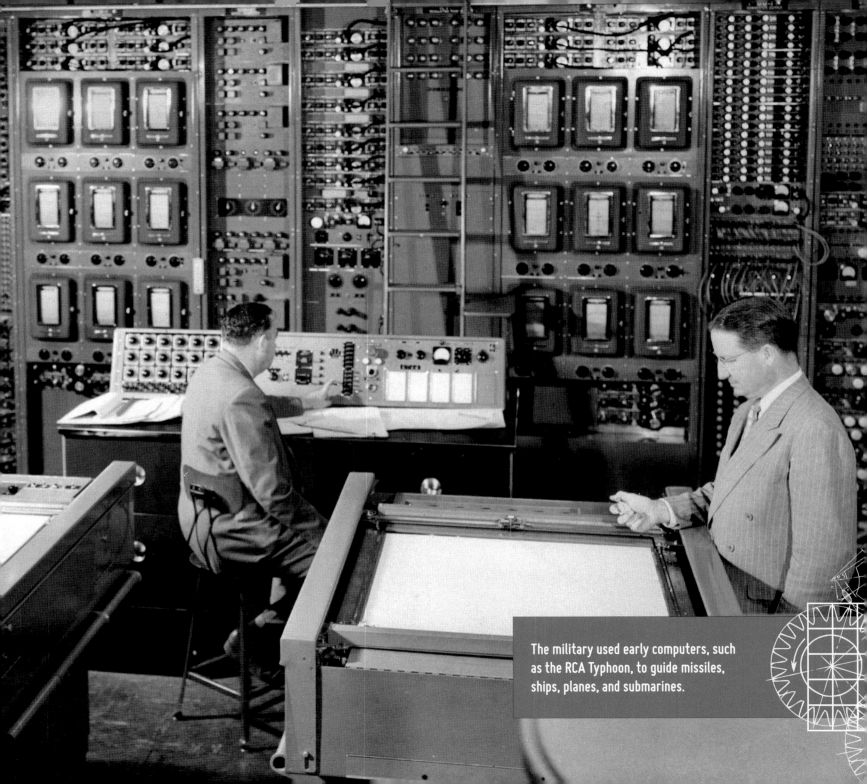

The military used early computers, such as the RCA Typhoon, to guide missiles, ships, planes, and submarines.

At that point in time, engineers could imagine and design electronics that could outperform anything previously designed. However, it was impossible to actually build them because the circuits, which are the basic building blocks of computer processors, would be too large and complex. A circuit with 100,000 parts needed 1 million soldered connections to link them together.[1] The only way to make those connections was by hand, so the labor and cost were unaffordable. This was called the "interconnections problem" or the "tyranny of numbers."[2] Unless someone found a solution to the problem, further technological advancement seemed impossible.

Finding a Solution

Countries such as the United Kingdom, France, the Soviet Union, and Germany worked hard to come up with a solution to the interconnections problems. In the United States, the military and private companies poured money into solving the problem, but none of the ideas worked.

JACK KILBY

Jack Kilby was born in 1923 and became an electrical engineer. In addition to developing the integrated circuit, he coinvented the first electronic handheld calculator and held patents for 60 other inventions. In 2000, he received the Nobel Prize for his work on the integrated circuit. He died in 2005.[3]

Computers were changing in the 1950s, but inventors were struggling to design a smaller and more affordable option.

Then, one summer day in 1958, engineer and inventor Jack Kilby was working alone in his office at Texas Instruments in Dallas, Texas. He had only recently started his job, and everyone else was on vacation, so the office was empty. Being alone in the office gave him plenty of time to think. In fact, Kilby was supposed to be working on a different task, but he started thinking about the interconnections problem. He began sketching and making notes, and he came up with the idea of putting all of the wires, resistors, and capacitors onto one chip to make a complete circuit. He developed the integrated circuit. Also called a chip, the integrated circuit was made of semiconductor material, and it was one-half the size of a paper clip. Although there were still some problems, the idea was revolutionary. No one previously had figured out how to eliminate all of the soldered connections required to make a circuit. The integrated circuit solved the interconnections problem.

Physical materials can be categorized by how well they conduct electricity. Conductors allow electricity to flow freely, whereas insulators do not. Semiconductors fall in the middle because they can conduct electricity or not, depending on how they are stimulated. They can be stimulated electrically, thermally (with heat), or physically. Common semiconductor materials are silicon and germanium. At first, germanium was the preferred material for computers because it was easier to work with than silicon. However, engineers realized silicon performed better, and by the end of the 1950s, silicon was the preferred material.

Another man, Robert Noyce, independently came up with his own idea for an integrated circuit a few months later. The parts were connected better than they were on Kilby's circuit, making it more appropriate for mass production. As a result of both men's work, smaller circuits could be made, manufacturing could be automated, and technologies could advance faster and further. Many of the electronics products we use today could not have been developed without the integrated circuit.

The history of the computer and its development is a story of many contributors building on previous work. Also, as with Jack Kilby, Robert Noyce, and the integrated circuit, several important stages of development occurred in which people worked on similar ideas, sometimes without realizing it until later.

Computers in Everyday Life

The effect of the integrated circuit breakthrough has been far reaching. Nowadays, computers are small, portable, and a part of virtually every aspect of daily life. But without the integrated circuit, that would not have been possible.

Laptops and tablets have become the norm in offices, schools, and homes. Watch a congested street, crowded bus, or busy coffee shop, and the majority of people are likely using a handheld computer called a smartphone.

ROBERT NOYCE

Robert Noyce is considered a coinventor of the integrated circuit. The company he cofounded, Fairchild Semiconductor, applied for a patent for the circuit. Jack Kilby's company had also applied, but Fairchild received the patent. Noyce later went on to cofound Intel Corporation, one of the largest manufacturers of integrated circuits in the world. Noyce was one of the first scientists to work in the area now called Silicon Valley and was nicknamed the "Mayor of Silicon Valley."[4] He died in 1990 at age 62.

THE INTEGRATED CIRCUIT IN SPACE

The integrated circuit and the Apollo space program, which started in 1961, had an important relationship. The Apollo Guidance Computer, which had an integrated circuit, helped navigate the spacecraft to the moon. Experts also say the need for better technology for the space program pushed faster advances for technology in everyday life. Because research and development of new technology is so expensive, some argue it might not have progressed so far and so fast without the financial input from NASA.

Whether using them to text, talk, or exchange e-mail, computers have become a foundation of communication throughout the world.

Computers are also embedded in everyday life in countless ways that may be less obvious. Many, if not most, household machines use computer technology. From washing machines to microwaves and remote controls, these devices incorporate computer technology. Outside of the house, a trip to the grocery store, getting cash from an ATM, or taking public transportation all involve computers too.

On a larger scale, computers are an integral part of fields such as medicine, business, and science. Consider a simple visit to the doctor's office where patient records are now computerized. Most medical tests involve a computer at some stage in the process. And computers now allow doctors to perform extremely delicate and complex surgeries. In business, computers are essential for record keeping and data processing. It would be almost unimaginable to think of an office or store without a computer. And the ways computers are involved in science would likely be impossible to count.

Computers are an important part of many industries, and many classrooms use computers daily.

THE SPEED OF INNOVATION

Moore's Law is often mentioned in relation to computer innovation. It is not actually a law. Gordon E. Moore is a cofounder of Intel Corporation. In the 1970s, he wrote a paper about his ideas on the speed of computer innovation. He believed processing speeds, or overall processing power of computers, would double every two years. This has proved true. However, some people in the technology industry question whether it will be true in the future. They believe the speed of innovation will increase and happen even faster.

There is no doubt, then, that computers have transformed our lives. And the speed and rate of this transformation can seem truly astounding. Since the development of the integrated circuit, components have been continuously improved. This has led to faster data processing and larger capacity for storing information on smaller and smaller computers, with a lower cost. As one writer expressed in 1996, "Today's computers are literally millions of times better than the first computers on almost all measures of this kind."[5] Presumably those millions in 1996 could be multiplied many times to describe the capacity of computers today.

THE COMPUTER

1931
Vannevar Bush's Differential Analyzer, an analog computer, is built.

1944
The Harvard Mark I is built.

1945
The ENIAC is built.

1947
The semiconductor transistor is invented.

1958
The integrated circuit is invented.

1971
The microprocessor is invented.

1975
Bill Gates and Paul Allen form Microsoft.

1977
Three of the first personal computers, the Apple II, Commodore PET, and TRS-80, come out.

1981
The IBM PC is released.

1984
The Apple Macintosh is introduced.

1985
Microsoft Windows 1.0 is released.

1993
The first smartphone, "Simon," is introduced.

2007
The Apple iPhone is introduced.

2008
The first Android phone is released.

2010
The Apple iPad is announced.

CHAPTER 2

EARLY
HISTORY

I t is difficult to pinpoint the date when the first computer was invented. If we think about the computer in terms of its functions—mathematical calculations and data processing—we can find precedents that go back centuries. If we think of the computer in terms of its technology—processors, memory, software, and input and output devices—most of the important inventions occurred in the 1900s. Some historians trace the origins of the computer back hundreds, if not thousands, of years. As long as humans have calculated numbers, they have looked for ways to make the process faster and easier.

Early computers in the 1930s were built to replace large calculating machines.

THE ANTIKYTHERA MECHANISM

In 1901, divers were exploring a shipwreck off the coast of Greece, near an island called Antikythera, when they found a mysterious object the size of a shoebox. The clocklike machine had more than 30 gears. Researchers call the device the Antikythera Mechanism. It has taken 100 years for scientists to confirm the mechanism was actually an early computer. They say the machine, which dates from approximately 100 BCE, was used to show astronomical positions and events.[1]

Early Calculating Devices

The abacus is one of the oldest calculating tools. It was used extensively in Europe and Asia for centuries, and it is still used today. An abacus has markers on a grid, and users move the markers to make calculations. Typical markers include stones, beads, coins, or sticks.

The slide rule was another calculating device. It was invented in the 1600s and used into the 1900s. The slide rule let the user do calculations such as multiplication and trigonometry. A slide rule has two bars marked with logarithmic scales that slide next to one another. Aligning the numbers on different kinds of scales allows for different types of calculations. It was practical for many tasks, but it was not always accurate. Accuracy depends on the quality of the slide rule and the user. For tasks that required accuracy, such as accounting or taking inventory, a mechanical calculator was better.

One of the earliest and most well known mechanical calculators was Napier's Bones. John Napier was a Scottish scientist and mathematician who created a system in 1617 that used a series of bones, or sticks, with numbers on them for multiplication. The idea for Napier's Bones may have originally come from the Middle East. A few years later, in approximately 1623, William Schickard added a tooth-wheeled system for addition and subtraction to Napier's Bones. It is the earliest known mechanical calculator. Schickard apparently built only two of the machines. The only record of the machines is in a letter from Schickard with sketches and a description of the calculator.

Blaise Pascal was also an important figure in the area of mechanical calculators. He was the son of a

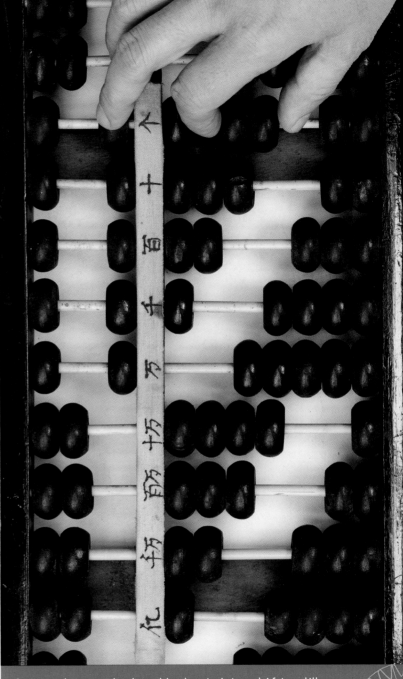

Some modern merchants and traders in Asia and Africa still use the abacus as a calculating tool.

tax collector and, in the 1640s, while he was still a teenager, he invented a machine that could add. The machine was called the Pascaline, and he built approximately 50 of them, which made it the first commercially produced machine. However, he sold only 15 of them.[2]

Beyond Numbers

Calculating devices helped people manipulate numbers, but what about processing other information such as words and ideas? The earliest answer for this was found in punched cards. Patterns of holes punched in cards could represent different kinds of information.

One of the first examples of punched cards was in France in the weaving industry. In 1804, Joseph-Marie Jacquard developed a loom that used punched cards to control the action of the loom and weave complex patterns into fabric. This automation was an important step in the Industrial Revolution. Because large sets of punched cards were bound in a program, it is often argued that this system is an ancestor of the modern computer.

It could take tens of thousands of individually punched cards to make an intricate pattern on a Jacquard Loom. The presence or absence of a hole in each position on a card programmed the loom to weave a particular pattern. After the cards were made, they could be reused to make identical patterns. The cards were essentially an early form of software. This made it possible for even beginning weavers to make valuable designs and fabric. It also meant rival weavers could steal the punch cards after they were created.

ADA LOVELACE

Ada Lovelace, who was the daughter of famous poet Lord Byron, studied mathematics, which was unusual for women in the 1800s. She became very interested in Babbage's machines. In 1843, she published a translation of a report about the Analytical Engine. She added extensive notes of her own, which included a description of a sequence of operations to solve certain mathematical problems. She was the first to clearly describe ideas about the machine's potential uses. She speculated the engine might be able to process other types of data, such as music or symbols, showing vision beyond even Babbage's ideas for his machine.

Babbage's Engines

In the early 1800s, several fields required large mathematical tables, which displayed the results of complex mathematical calculations, such as logarithms. Instead of doing these calculations themselves, users would simply look up the answer in a published table. For example, Great Britain, and later the United States, needed reliable tables for navigation at sea. The only way to produce those tables was by human calculation, which was an enormous task. And the tables often had errors in them. Charles Babbage was an English mathematician and computer pioneer. Frustrated with all the errors in an astronomy table, he decided to try to build a machine that could do the calculations for tables without all the mistakes.

Babbage's first planned machine was the Difference Engine, which was for calculating and tabulating large numbers. Until then, calculations were rarely done to more than six digits, but Babbage planned to use his machine to make calculations with results up to 20 or 30 digits long.[3] Babbage managed to secure government grants to fund his project. An engineer began working on the engine in 1821 but stopped in 1833 after a dispute with Babbage. The engine was never built, and it was a very expensive failure. Babbage managed to complete a small prototype of his Difference Engine. Although it could not be used for table making, Babbage used it to demonstrate his ideas on computing, and it showed his idea was feasible.

After his first engine failed, Babbage came up with the idea for an even more advanced

The first complete Babbage engine was built in London in 2002, 153 years after its design. It has 8,000 parts, weighs 5 short tons (4.5 metric tons), and is 11 feet (3.4 m) long.[4]

The prototype of the Difference Machine is still on display in London's Science Museum.

COMPUTER LOGIC PIONEER

English mathematician George Boole developed a system of logic called *Boolean Logic*. In 1847, Boole argued that all ideas can be expressed very simply. First, according to Boole, all statements are either true or false. Then, it is possible to combine more than one of the statements with AND, OR, and NOT. It was not clear what practical use his ideas had for decades. Then in the 1930s, computer scientist Claude Shannon learned about Boolean's idea and realized it could have real world application. Boolean logic is now a foundation for modern digital computers because it fits with the binary system used. In a binary system, each bit has a value of either 0 or 1. Or, according to Boolean Logic, each bit is either true or false.

machine. This was later called the Analytical Engine. Similar to the Jacquard Loom, this engine used punched cards to program. The design included functions that are part of the modern digital computer. For example, the punched cards allowed users to input numbers. There was a function Babbage called the *store*, which was where numbers could be stored before and during processing, making it the machine's memory. The *mill* was where the calculations happened, which is comparable to a processing unit. Finally, the Analytical Engine had a printing device to output results. If the machine had been built, it would have been much larger than the Difference Engine. And, because it required hand cranking to process data, it would have required strength that might not have been physically possible for even the strongest human.

Babbage never managed to build his Analytical Engine. However, because of the features of his design, many people consider Babbage a computer pioneer. As one writer states, "Babbage's machine, was, at least on paper, a true predecessor of modern computers."[5]

The Curta Calculator was a small pocket calculator that could add, subtract, multiply, and divide, among other functions.

The Curta Calculator is a mechanical calculator designed by Curt Herzstark in the 1940s. Herzstark was imprisoned in Buchenwald concentration camp during World War II (1939–1945). He thought about his design while he was imprisoned, and then he finished the design after he was freed. His Curta Calculator was introduced in 1948. At the time, the calculator, which could perform addition, subtraction, multiplication, and division, was the smallest four-function calculator ever built. This impressive device is still studied and valued by collectors.

CHAPTER 3

FROM PEOPLE TO MACHINES

Today, the word *computer* describes a machine, one that sits on our desks or is carried around and performs a myriad of functions. However, the word originally described a person, someone who did computations and solved equations. Using the word to describe a machine only started around 1945. Until the end of the 1800s and into the 1900s, humans performed the work that computers do today, from calculations to data processing.

The Electric Tabulating System

In the 1800s, the largest and most important data processing office in the United States was the Bureau of the Census. The first

A US Navy technician controls an early calculating machine called the Automatic Sequence.

THE MECHANICAL TIDE PREDICTOR

In 1872, Lord Kelvin, a British scientist, invented a mechanical tide predictor. This was an important example of analog computing technology. Tide tables could help minimize danger to ships when they entered harbors, but making tables was time-consuming, so they were made only for a few major ports. Lord Kelvin's predictor used wires, pulleys, shafts, and gear wheels that replicated gravitational forces on the sea. It charted water levels in a harbor on paper. Tide tables could be created from the high and low points the machine traced on the paper. Copies of the predictor were built and used for ports around the world. New and improved models were built and used until the 1950s, when the predictors were replaced by digital computers.

population census was done in 1790, with a US population estimate of 3.9 million, but no records remain to explain how it was carried out. Between 1840 and 1880, the number of census clerks went from 28 to at least 1,495. It took seven years to process the information from the 1880 census.[1] This was too long, and there was strong motivation to find a faster way.

The US government held a contest to find a solution. Herman Hollerith, a young engineer, won. His idea was to record population data on punched cards. With Hollerith's Electric Tabulating System, clerks were able to process approximately 7,000 cards a day.[2] This was ten times faster than the previous method by hand. In the end, the 1890 census information was processed in two and a half years, instead of the seven years of the previous census.

After his success with the census, Hollerith focused on selling his machine to businesses. He started the Tabulating Machine Company

(TMC) and produced a range of machines for business use. Eventually, he sold the business and became a rich man. After the sale, TMC merged with another company and became part of the Computing-Tabulating-Recording Company (C-T-R). In 1924, that company became the well-known business machine and computer company International Business Machines (IBM).

Analog Computers

Before digital computers, there were analog computers. Analog computers use mechanical motion or the flow of electricity to model problems and produce answers. The slide rule is a simple analog calculator. Analog computers can be either mechanical or electronic.

Herman Hollerith's tabulating machine read the pattern of holes on the punched cards, speeding up the census clerks' jobs.

VANNEVAR BUSH AND THE MEMEX

Vannevar Bush wrote a magazine article in 1945 with his ideas about how scientists could access and use all of the knowledge available to humans. In the article, he describes something he calls a memex. Bush said, "A memex is a device in which an individual stores all his books, records, and communications, and which is mechanized so that it may be consulted with exceeding speed and flexibility."[3] Bush also describes the memex as a device that could supplement human memory and imitate the way the human mind makes associations between ideas. Many people see these ideas as a direct forerunner to modern hypertext links and even as inspiration for the World Wide Web.

One of the key figures in analog computing was Vannevar Bush. In 1931, he built a machine called the Differential Analyzer. This was a mechanical analog computer, with a complicated combination of gears, levers, belts, and shafts, and it filled an entire room. The Differential Analyzer was intended to model power transmission networks, but Bush realized the machine had potential for other uses. The analyzer was used to solve physics, seismology, and ballistics problems. It could solve extremely complex equations, but it had to be set up for each new problem, which was difficult. As a result of Bush's work, many similar machines were built around the world. Bush made a more advanced version of the machine called the Rockefeller Differential Analyzer in 1935.

Analog computers developed further after the Differential Analyzer. During World War II, electronic analog computers were built that gave the machines faster computing speeds. Electronic analog computers work on the same principles as mechanical ones, but they

Vannevar Bush helped push the development of the computer forward with his work in the 1930s.

COMPUTER CATEGORIES

Computers are generally divided into two categories: analog and digital. Analog computers use mechanical motion and the flow of electricity to model problems and provide answers. Analog data is of a continuous nature; an analog system is set up according to initial conditions and then allowed to change freely. A digital computer processes data in discrete form. Data, including numbers, letters, and magnitudes, is expressed in binary form. *Binary* means that all data is represented using only the two digits 0 and 1. A digital computer counts, compares, and manipulates combinations of those digits to perform all its tasks.

use electric components instead of physical ones. This makes it easier to change them for new problems because it is not always necessary to change the physical parts. Analog computers for engineering and scientific calculation continued to be used into the 1950s. However, it was clear analog computing was not enough. For problems where it was not possible to make a physical or electric model, something else was needed.

Electronic and Digital

From the 1930s on, more and more fields of study required large-scale calculations. Human computers and punched card machines were used, but the process was still slow and difficult. Between 1935 and 1945, several inventors around the world were creating calculators that could work faster. In most cases, the inventors were working without knowledge of others' work along similar lines. The result was that several different machines were built during this period.

Howard Aiken tweaks a knob on the Mark I machine before presenting his invention to Harvard University.

AIKEN AND BABBAGE

Howard Aiken had never heard of Charles Babbage when he got his idea for the Mark I machine. While Aiken was working to get funding for his project, someone showed him a small fragment of one of Babbage's engines that was stored in an attic at Harvard University. Aiken got inspiration from Babbage's concept, and the Mark I was described as "Babbage's Dream Come True." The Mark I was possibly only ten times faster than what Babbage imagined for his engine. Within only two years of the Mark I, computers were developed that were thousands of times faster.[4]

The most well known of these machines was the IBM Automatic Sequence Controlled Calculator, which was more commonly called the Harvard Mark I. Howard Aiken, a researcher at Harvard University in Massachusetts, wanted to improve on Bush's Differential Analyzer and build a large-scale digital calculator. Sponsored by IBM, Aiken built the

TURING AND THE UNIVERSAL COMPUTING MACHINE

British mathematician Alan Turing is sometimes called the "father of the modern computer." In 1936, Turing wrote about his idea for a "universal computing machine," which is now referred to as the Turing Machine.[6] His idea was to control the computer's operations by a program of coded instructions, which would be stored in the computer's memory. As a result, the machine would be able to carry out any task. In 1936, this idea was revolutionary. Turing hoped to actually build such a machine, but he never did. He soon went to work on machines that broke German military codes in World War II.

machine and ran its first test problem in 1943. The machine was huge, and one person described the machine as sounding like "a roomful of ladies knitting."[5] The Mark I was relatively slow, even by standards then, but it was important because it was the first fully automatic calculating machine. Once it was started, it could run for hours or even days. More advanced versions of the Mark (Mark II, III, and IV) were built later.

In Germany in 1936, civil engineering student Konrad Zuse started working on a mechanical computer at home. He used metal plates, pins, and old movie film to make a machine called the Z1. He was working alone, but he developed a machine with features of later computers, such as use of a binary system and being programmable. In Iowa, mathematics and physics professor John Atanasoff and graduate student Clifford Berry built an electronic computing device called the Atanasoff-Berry Computer (ABC). The ABC was completed in 1941, and it is considered to have been the first electronic digital computer. It was relatively unknown for decades because it was not patented.

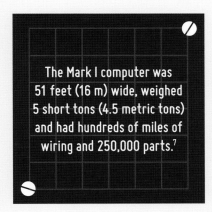

The Mark I computer was 51 feet (16 m) wide, weighed 5 short tons (4.5 metric tons) and had hundreds of miles of wiring and 250,000 parts.[7]

During World War II, teams of engineers and mathematicians, including Alan Turing, worked at Bletchley Park, the British Government Code and Cypher School. Their goal was to break codes that would give information about enemy plans and movements. One of the machines they made was the Colossus, which was an all-electronic computer used to break code. Some estimates suggest the Colossus, along with other code-breaking machines, shortened the war by at least two years. The computer was also an important step in computer development, but almost no one knew about its existence until after 1970 because it was classified information.

CHAPTER 4

CALCULATING MACHINES

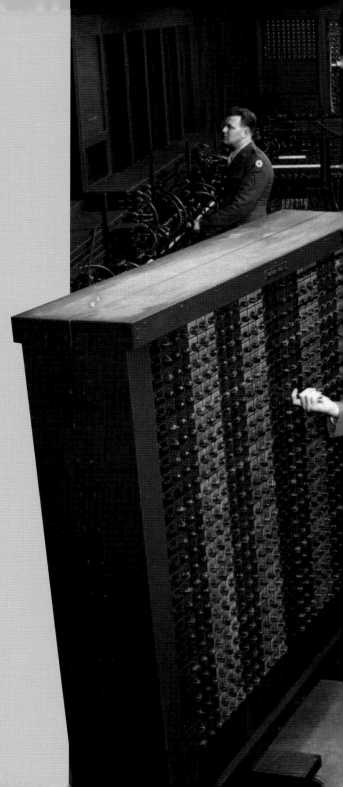

World War II pushed computer development by providing military funding, recruiting people for computing projects, and creating a sense of urgency for constant research and development. Bush's Differential Analyzer, the Harvard Mark I, and many human calculators were used, but they were not efficient enough.

Physicist John Mauchly proposed an all-electronic calculating machine. Mauchly worked with engineer J. Presper Eckert. Built between 1943 and 1945 at the University of Pennsylvania's Moore School of Electrical Engineering, the Electronic Numerical Integrator and Computer (ENIAC) was more complex than any electronic

Mauchly and his team work on the ENIAC machine at the Moore School of Electrical Engineering.

system built previously. The machine filled an entire room and weighed almost 30 short tons (27 metric tons).[1] In the ten years it was in use, the ENIAC perhaps ran more calculations than all humankind combined had done up to that point.

Circuits are the basic building blocks of computer processors. A circuit is opened or closed by a switch; in other words, it switches between the two states of "off" and "on." Previous computers such as the Harvard Mark I had used electromechanical relays for their switches. Because the relays physically move to open and close, these switches were relatively slow. However, the ENIAC used vacuum tubes for its switches. A vacuum tube is an electronic switch. Electronic switches rely on the much faster movement of electrons to complete the circuit. As a result, the ENIAC was much faster than the Mark I. Whereas the Mark I could perform a few additions per second, the ENIAC could perform 5,000 additions per second.

There were problems with the ENIAC, though. The vacuum tubes used were approximately the size of a standard light bulb today and more than 17,000 of them were used in the ENIAC.[2] Vacuum tubes wear out and need to be changed. With more than 17,000 tubes, that meant a lot of work. With time, maintenance teams got better at fixing problems quickly, but it was still challenging.

John Mauchly, *left*, worked with engineer J. Presper Eckert, *right*, to design and build the ENIAC.

Stored-Program Computers

Computers need to be given instructions to perform tasks; this is known as *programming*. One challenge in programming is finding an easy and effective way to express these instructions. This led to the development of various programming languages. A more basic challenge was how to physically input the programmer's instructions into the machine. With Mark I, instructions were fed in using punched cards, but card readers were too slow for the much faster ENIAC. Instead, programmers would rewire the ENIAC's various components together using cables similar to a telephone switchboard. This allowed the computer to run quickly, but it was time-consuming to set up. Reprogramming ENIAC for each new problem could take hours, if not days.

To speed up the programming process, Eckert and Mauchly began thinking about an alternative to physically rewiring the machine: storing the program instructions within the machine's memory. This meant the program would not have to be fed into the computer as it was running. The famous mathematician John von Neumann got involved with the project and then went on to help design an improved computer called the Electronic Discrete Variable Automated Computer (EDVAC). In his widely read EDVAC report of 1945, von Neumann elaborated on the stored-program concept and helped popularize it. A stored-program computer stores program instructions in electronic memory. This gives the computer more flexibility to perform various tasks in sequence. Von Neumann also used binary to represent numbers, rather than the decimal numbers that had been used in ENIAC. The EDVAC was not completed until the early 1950s.

COMPUTER PATENT

The inventors of the ENIAC applied for patents in 1947 and received them in 1964. However, there were objections. One of the biggest issues was that Mauchly had visited Atanasoff and seen his ABC computer in 1941 before starting work on the ENIAC. The disagreement went to court. The ruling recognized Atanasoff's work and took away the patents. As a result, no one has a patent for the first electronic computer.

The first stored-program computer built was completed at Manchester University in England. It was nicknamed the Baby, and it was finished in 1948. The first program it ran

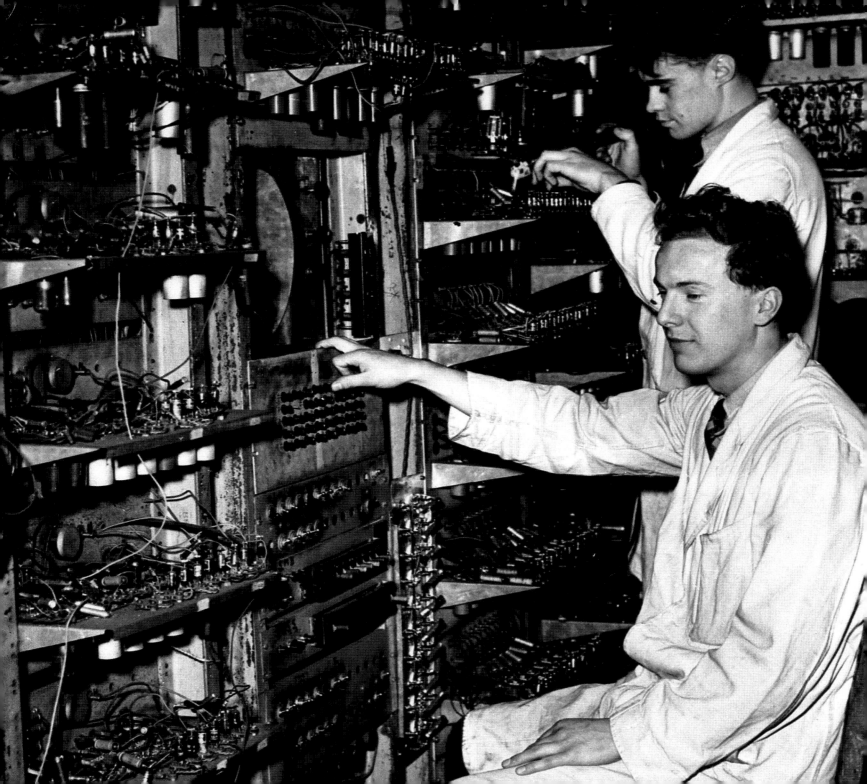

had 17 instructions and ran for 52 minutes.[4] The Baby was only a demonstration machine, but by 1949 the team at Manchester University had built a full-scale version called the Manchester Mark I.

The Electronic Delay Storage Automatic Calculator (EDSAC), which was built at Cambridge University in England, followed the Baby and it ran its first programs in 1949. Maurice Wilkes, a physicist at Cambridge, was inspired by von Neumann's designs for the EDVAC. The EDSAC become the first stored-program computer to be used regularly.

Once the stored-program computer had been developed, universities and research labs around the world wanted one. Von Neumann, who was based at Princeton University, suggested the university's Institute for Advanced Studies (IAS) build its own stored-program computer. The computer was completed in 1951. IAS made the design for the computer available to anyone. As a result, there were similar machines built around the world.

The Commercial Market

Until this point, computers had mainly been developed to process numbers and mathematical equations for government and military purposes. The stored-program concept was a huge advance, but there were no commercial manufacturers. The only way to get a computer was to build one. People began thinking about making and selling

The Baby filled an entire lab at Manchester University.

GRACE HOPPER

Grace Hopper was a mathematician, teacher, and a computer pioneer. She joined the US Naval Reserve during World War II and was assigned to work on the Mark I project at Harvard University. After the war, she worked on the UNIVAC project. In 1951, Hopper created the first compiler: a program that translated the human-readable instructions created by programmers into the binary code needed by the machine. She went on to create the first business programming language in 1952. This work led to the development of Common Business Oriented Language (COBOL), a programming language for businesses that was widely used for many decades and is still used in some places today.

computers commercially, but no one knew how big the market might be or what kind of risks might be involved in the business.

After their work on ENIAC, Mauchly and Eckert started a company and began work on a series of computers, the most successful of which was called the Universal Automatic Computer (UNIVAC). They were contracted to make the computer for the US Bureau of the Census in 1946, and the UNIVAC passed Census Bureau tests to make sure it worked properly in 1951. A major innovation with the computer was the use of a magnetic tape drive, called the Uniservo, which read and wrote data ten times faster than punched cards did. The computer was also accurate. One Census Bureau official said, "We have never found it in error."[5] After this success, the UNIVAC was then manufactured for other users, becoming the first commercial computer in the world.

Early computer companies were already in the office equipment and telecommunications business. A move into selling computers

UNIVAC ON TV

In 1952, UNIVAC had a great publicity moment. The CBS television network was persuaded to use the computer to predict the outcome of the presidential election between Dwight D. Eisenhower and Adlai Stevenson. Polls before Election Day suggested a close race. Mauchly created a program for UNIVAC that would use early voting returns from key states to predict the results of the election. Very quickly, the computer predicted a big victory for Eisenhower. It seemed unbelievable that the computer could accurately predict this based on so few votes. The UNIVAC operators decided to change the parameters of the program to produce more believable results. It turned out the computer had been correct. Eisenhower won with 442 electoral votes to 89 for Stevenson. This was extremely close to the computer's early prediction of 438 to 93.[6]

seemed logical for these companies. The success of the UNIVAC machine was a wake up call for IBM. The company had been focused on building large calculators for the government for defense purposes. After the publicity UNIVAC got during the 1952 presidential election, IBM leaders realized they needed to adjust their focus. They started working to transform their product line.

CHAPTER 5

THE SECOND GENERATION

In the early 1950s, most computers used vacuum tube technology, but there were problems. Vacuum tubes were also unreliable. If one tube stopped working, it shut down the whole system until the problem tube could be found and replaced. A solution was needed.

Physicist William Shockley worked for Bell Labs in New York City. Working with John Bardeen and Walter Brattain, the three made the first transistor in 1947. A transistor, which is made of semiconductor material, is commonly used to amplify or switch electronic signals. In 1948, Shockley invented a better transistor. Transistors were significantly smaller than vacuum tubes, used very little power,

Vacuum tubes in early computers took up
a lot of space and used a lot of power.

COMPUTER GAMES

The idea of computer games appeared early in the development of computers. At the University of Cambridge in England in 1952, Sandy Douglas made the first graphical computer game, which was a kind of ticktacktoe game. In 1958, William Higinbotham created a game called Tennis for Two. It was an electronic tennis game where two players used separate controllers connected to a computer. He thought a game could help make science seem more relevant to everyday life. In 1962, a game called Spacewar! was created. In the game, two players operate spaceships and fire torpedoes at the opponent. All three of these games are predecessors to modern computer games.

and were reliable. However, they were expensive. A transistor cost approximately $20, compared with $1 for a vacuum tube.[1] Still, the invention of the transistor was a major step toward smaller and cheaper computers. The computers that used transistors, instead of vacuum tubes, are often called the second generation.

At first, because of their cost, transistors were mainly used in small consumer products such as hearing aids and radios in which vacuum tubes could not be used. In 1954, engineers from Bell Labs built the first computer without vacuum tubes, called Transistorized Digital Computer (TRADIC), for the US military. It was significantly smaller than the ENIAC. In terms of speed, it was similar to a vacuum tube computer, but it used very little power in comparison.

The US Air Force wanted a lighter-weight computer for use in their planes. The TRADIC computer fit their needs.

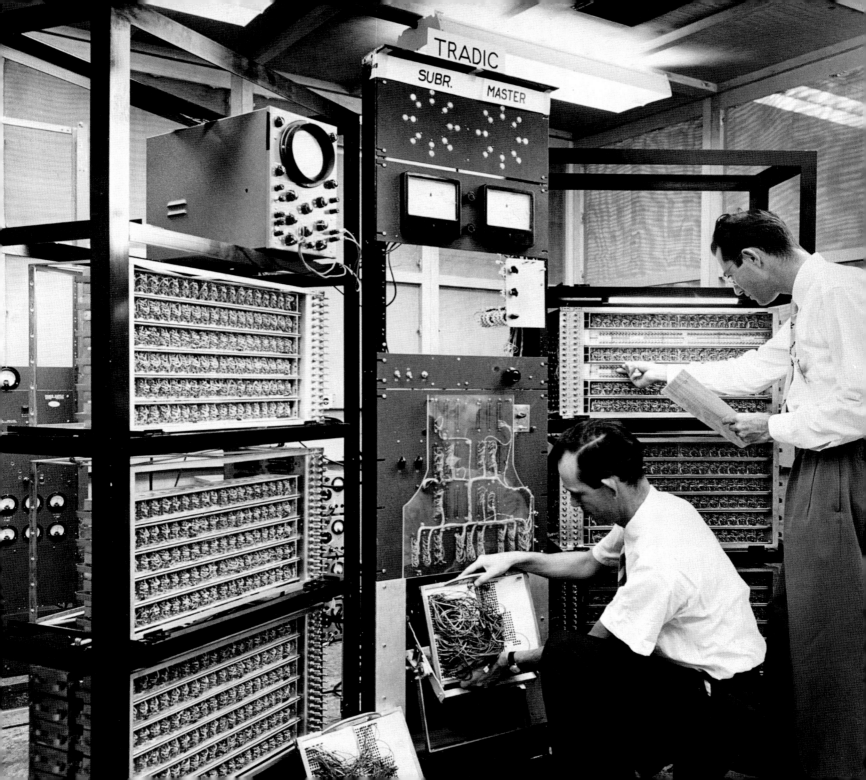

Silicon Valley and the Integrated Circuit

In 1955, Shockley left Bell Labs and started his own company in Mountain View, California. However, he was a difficult manager, and eight of his employees left soon after to form their own transistor company called Fairchild Semiconductor. The eight scientists, called the "traitorous eight," included Robert Noyce who would become a coinventor of the integrated circuit.[2] These companies were some of the first in the area that is now called Silicon Valley.

After they had coinvented the integrated circuit, Jack Kilby and Robert Noyce took the work in somewhat different directions. Kilby, who worked for Texas Instruments, was asked to make a calculator that could fit in a pocket. At the time, calculators were large, desktop, electromechanical machines. Kilby coinvented an electronic, handheld calculator. This was significant because it helped commercialize the integrated circuit. Noyce and Fairchild Semiconductor made integrated circuits for government contracts.

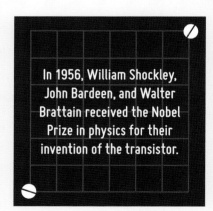

In 1956, William Shockley, John Bardeen, and Walter Brattain received the Nobel Prize in physics for their invention of the transistor.

Mainframes

Computers in the 1950s were large machines called mainframes. As companies became more aware of the computer's potential to help them in their business, they wanted flexible, large-scale machines that could combine a variety of tasks. Mainframe computers gave companies this flexibility. There were many computer manufacturers, but IBM dominated the market.

Manufacturers were making computers for different uses, from science to data processing in business. The problem was the computers were incompatible. They all used different software, which made it complicated for everyone involved. IBM held secret meetings to make a plan to deal with this issue. They came up with the idea to make all of their computers run the same programs and use the same disks, tapes, and printers. They created the System/360, which was one unified system. It was very successful, and every IBM mainframe made since is a descendant of the original. Competitors to IBM came out with their own mainframes, but none were as successful.

THE END OF THE MAINFRAME . . . OR NOT

As computer technology has advanced, many people have predicted the end of the mainframe. In 1991, technology writer Stewart Alsop said, "I predict the last mainframe will be unplugged on March 15, 1996."[4] In 2001, he admitted he had been wrong. Mainframes are still used, especially by banks and for airline reservations.

Although mainframe computers were useful for businesses in many ways, they took up large amounts of space.

Minicomputers

A class of computers called "minicomputers" emerged in the early 1960s. A mainframe could cost as much as $1 million. It was also large and usually required specialized technicians to operate. As the name suggests, a minicomputer was smaller and usually was more general purpose. It offered a whole new set of possible uses, including accounting for small businesses, collecting scientific data, or controlling manufacturing. Compared with the high price of a mainframe, a minicomputer was also less expensive, with a price tag of less than $100,000 depending on the model.[5]

One of the most popular and best-selling minicomputers was the PDP-8 made by Digital Equipment Corporation (DEC). The PDP line of computers was created after the Canadian Chalk River Nuclear Lab needed a special machine to monitor a nuclear reactor. The expected approach was to build a custom machine for the job. However, the DEC engineers took a different approach. They built a small, general-purpose computer and programmed it to do the job of monitoring the reactor.

Nearly 100 companies were making minicomputers at one point in the late 1960s.[6] The competition increased innovation and lowered prices, which resulted in more companies choosing to use computers. In the end, most of these computer companies did not survive, but a few continued making minicomputers until personal computers (PCs) became common.

THE KITCHEN COMPUTER

Before computers became the norm at home, there did not seem to be a lot of possible uses for them there. However, the upscale department store Neiman–Marcus had a suggestion. The cover for their 1969 Christmas catalog featured the Kitchen Computer, which could be used to store recipes. With a price tag of $10,600, the buyer would get the computer, a cookbook, an apron, and a two-week programming course. No Kitchen Computers were ever sold.[7]

HOW A COMPUTER WORKS

A computer is a machine that processes data, or information. It takes in the data, stores it as needed, changes or processes it, and then puts out the information at the end. These steps are referred to by some common names.

Computer hardware refers to the devices that are fixed and solid, such as the computer itself and the monitor. It also includes the keyboard, mouse, and printer. Inside the computer are other pieces of hardware, including the motherboard, which is the main circuit board of the computer and contains the central processing unit (CPU) and various types of memory.

There are two main types of memory: random access memory (RAM) and read-only memory (ROM). RAM is short-term and temporary. It remembers only what the computer is working on while the power is on. The data is not permanently stored when the power goes off. In contrast, ROM is built-in memory. As the name *read-only* suggests, data stored in ROM can only be read. It either cannot be modified, or it can only be changed with difficulty. Unlike RAM, ROM keeps what it is storing even when the power is off.

Software is the many programs installed on a computer to perform different activities. Software gives a computer flexibility to carry out the tasks a user might want to do. There is operating system software, the core system in the computer that controls the basic functions the computer performs. Applications software is another type of program used for specific tasks. For example, a word processing program, a game, and an accounting program are all different applications.

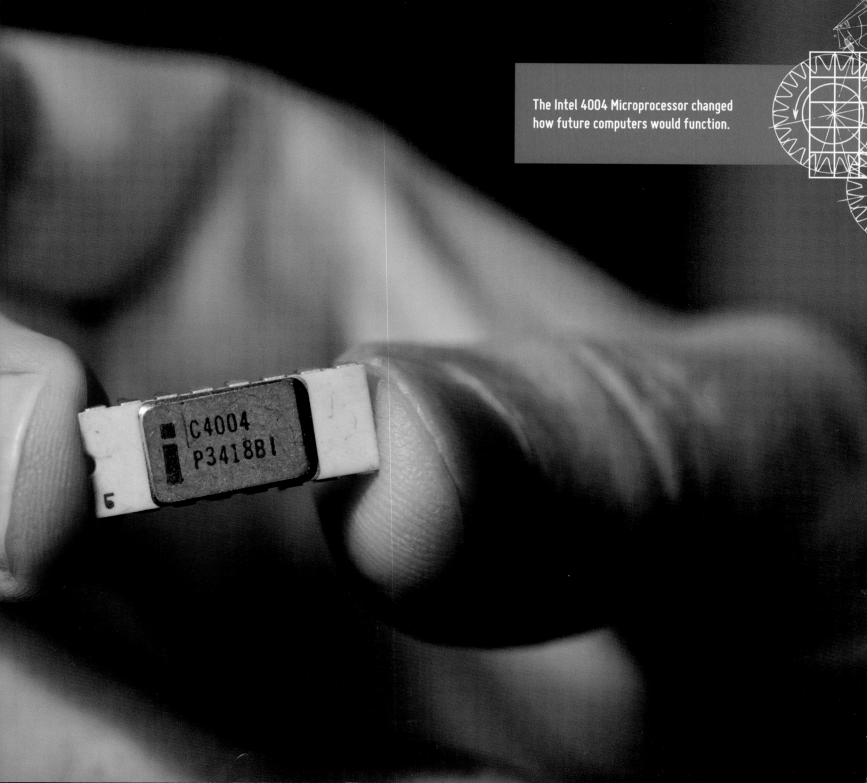

The Intel 4004 Microprocessor changed how future computers would function.

C4004
P3418B1

calculators asked Intel to make a line of chips with different capabilities. Hoff was assigned the job. He decided that, rather than making different chips for these different functions, it would be more efficient to design a general-purpose chip that could be programmed with different functions. Essentially, the one chip would be a basic computer. It would have all of the functions of a tiny, general-purpose, stored-program computer. Everything needed to run the computer's programs, remember information, and manage data could be contained on one chip. So in 1971, the microprocessor, named the Intel 4004 Microprocessor, was born. Intel advertised it as "a computer on a chip."[1]

The Role of Hobbyists

The invention of the microprocessor was a major innovation, and it eventually revolutionized many activities of daily life for consumers. It also opened the door to the development of the PC. The people who contributed most to this development were hobbyists. These were people who were interested in electronics and enjoyed trying to put together their own machines. They worked in basements, garages, and dorm rooms.

Minicomputers were still relatively expensive, costing as much as $20,000 for complete installation.[2] However, hobbyists were willing to do the work needed to make computers more practical and accessible to an individual. Electronics magazines were a source of

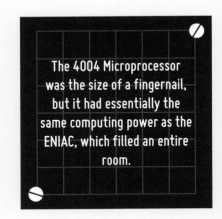

The 4004 Microprocessor was the size of a fingernail, but it had essentially the same computing power as the ENIAC, which filled an entire room.

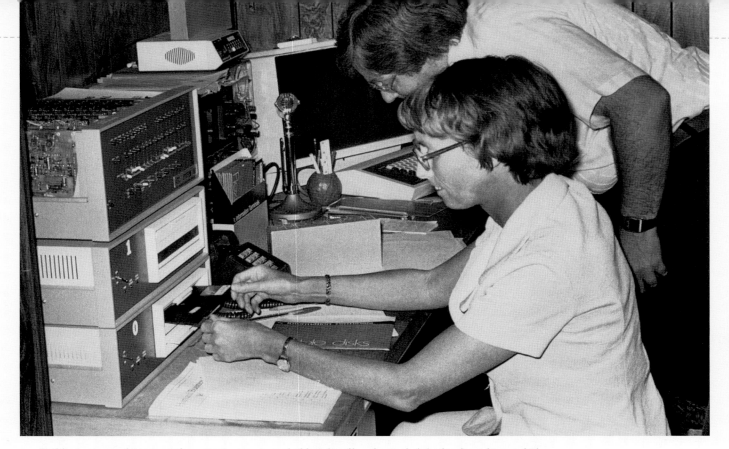

Building a computer was not an easy process, so hobbyists often formed clubs to share tips and ideas.

ideas, information, and inspiration. Articles might give instructions or describe devices that could be useful. Magazines also gave information about where to buy parts and equipment. There were also kits hobbyists could buy to assemble a computer themselves.

CLEAN ROOMS AND BUNNY SUITS

Microprocessors need to be manufactured in an extremely clean environment to protect the intricate devices from any contamination. Technicians wear protective clothing, commonly called "bunny suits," to protect the chips. Early versions of the bunny suits were less complex, but nowadays, a suit includes gloves, a hood with a filter, and protective footwear. Workers also pass through an air shower to decontaminate before they enter the clean room. In 1997, Intel ran a commercial showing chip manufacturing technicians dancing to pop music in colorful bunny suits. As a result of the commercial, there were even "bunny people" dolls made.

The Altair 8800

Several computers could be called the first PC. The first popular computer available by kit was the Altair 8800. The magazine *Popular Electronics* had a prototype of the Altair on the cover of its January 1975 issue. Ed Roberts who was the owner of Micro Instrumentation Telemetry Systems (MITS), designed the computer. The Altair sold for $400.[3] The buyer had to put it together, make it work, and write any necessary software.

The only way to program the Altair was by entering instructions in binary code using hand switches on the front. This limited the machine to a small number of programs. Bill Gates and Paul Allen were immediately interested in the Altair because they thought that developing and selling software for computers could be a profitable business. They proposed developing a software system to Roberts. Gates and Allen created a partnership called Micro-Soft and spent six weeks developing Beginner's All-purpose Symbolic Instruction Code (BASIC). BASIC is a computer programming language developed in 1964. Gates and Allen developed the software to make the Altair run BASIC. This is how Microsoft (the hyphen was eventually dropped) was born.

Copying and sharing software was commonplace in the late 1970s. Gates quickly challenged that view, and he argued programmers and software developers should receive more money for their work. In 1976, he wrote an open letter to computer hobbyists, criticizing early software users for sharing, rather than paying for, software. By 1978, Microsoft's year-end sales were more than $1 million.[4] This showed some people were willing to buy software, rather than just share it.

Thousands of people bought the Altair 8000 kit designed by Roberts, making it a huge success.

The Age of Personal Computers

The next few years marked a dramatic and innovative time as microcomputers moved from being only for hobbyists to becoming a general consumer product. Two other important names in computer history, Steve Wozniak and Steve Jobs, started working on their own version of a microcomputer. In 1976, the Apple I was offered for sale for $666.66.[5] It was a simple computer with 4K of RAM and BASIC programming language on a cassette. It did not include a power supply, storage system, display, or keyboard. They sold approximately 200 Apple I microcomputers.[6] Wozniak and Jobs put each Apple I microcomputer together by hand in Jobs's parents' garage.

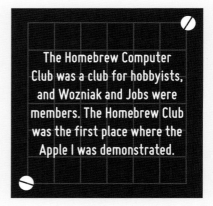

The Homebrew Computer Club was a club for hobbyists, and Wozniak and Jobs were members. The Homebrew Club was the first place where the Apple I was demonstrated.

The age of a PC for the mass market really arrived in 1977, when three different machines were released within a few months. Sometimes called the trinity, they included the Commodore Personal Electronic Transactor (PET), the Tandy Radio Shack TRS-80, and the Apple II. The PET had a small, calculator-like keyboard and was not as successful as the others. The TRS-80 was not as advanced as the Apple II, but it was half the price, which made it attractive to consumers. The Apple II already had the style and user-friendly feel Apple computers have become known for. It had a full keyboard, a floppy disk drive, and the spreadsheet program VisiCalc. Unlike earlier computers, the user did not have

Steve Wozniak, *left*, and Steve Jobs, *right*, started Apple in the 1970s, unaware of how big their company would become.

to supply any basic parts, which was revolutionary. The Apple II was the most expensive of the three PCs at $1,298, but it lasted the longest and sold the most.[7]

The PC and Clones

IBM now recognized the new market for PCs and reacted quickly, releasing the IBM PC within approximately one year. In the past, many of its products had taken three years to reach the market. Some components were original

THE FLOPPY DISK

Engineers at IBM invented the floppy disk in 1971. It was called a "memory disk" when it first came out, but it later became known as a "floppy disk" because it was made of flexible plastic. Computer data was written onto and read from the disk's surface. The first disk was 8 inches (20 cm) in diameter.[8] It was revolutionary because it was portable and could transfer data from one computer to another. Recordable CDs, DVDs, and flash drives later replaced floppies.

designs, but because IBM wanted to move quickly, it also used existing IBM products and components from other manufacturers to build the machine. Also, and probably most significant for IBM, was the decision to use the Intel 8088 processor with the Microsoft operating system, MS-DOS.

MS-DOS stands for Microsoft Disk Operating System. An operating system is the most important software that runs on a computer because it manages the computer's memory, processes, and all of its software and hardware. Before developing it for IBM, Microsoft had never actually written an operating system before. Microsoft bought the QDOS, or the Quick and Dirty Operating System, written by Tim Paterson of Seattle Computer Products. MS-DOS was based on QDOS.

The release of the IBM PC in 1981 was a huge success, which ensured the success of Intel. Also as a result, MS-DOS became the world's principal operating system. Although it was not the first computer to be called a PC, PC quickly became the name used for the IBM machine, as well as future imitators.

Very shortly afterward, other companies, including Dell and Compaq, began releasing PC-compatible computers. Gates had sold IBM the rights to one of his operating systems for its PC, but he kept the rights to a very similar version for Microsoft. As a result, when other manufacturers started making PC clones, they could use Microsoft's software for the operating system. Similarly, manufacturers could buy and use the Intel microprocessor in their products. IBM's PCs were higher-priced because of the status of the IBM brand. Unfortunately for IBM, consumers soon realized that, because the components were basically the same, they could get the same product at a lower price by buying an IBM imitator. This eventually took its toll, and IBM lost its dominance in the market.

Apple and GUI

PCs were dominating the market, but Steve Jobs had made a commitment to creating user-friendly computers. Jobs did not believe

APPLICATIONS SOFTWARE

Until 1977, there were not many software firms. Microsoft, with its BASIC programming language, was one of the few software companies at that point. However, the demand for applications software increased dramatically as individual users bought computers. The three main markets were games, education, and business. The first business application with wide success was VisiCalc. A Harvard MBA student named Daniel Bricklin wanted to enable an individual to use a PC for financial analysis, which is why he developed VisiCalc. It could be bought with the Apple II, and it was an instant success.

PCs were as easy to use for the average person as they could be, so it became his personal mission to develop a truly user-friendly computer. He had visited the Palo Alto Research Center (PARC), which was a division of the Xerox Corporation, where he got inspiration for Apple's next product. One of the research projects he saw at PARC was called the Xerox Alto. With most computers built in the 1970s, users had to type in text commands. On the Xerox Alto, users moved small picture icons around with a computer mouse. The Xerox Alto was the first use of a graphical user interface (GUI). Jobs was amazed by what he saw. Computer scientist Larry Tesler, who worked there at the time, showed Jobs the machines and reports him saying, "Why isn't Xerox marketing this? . . . You could blow everybody away!"[9]

Jobs went back to Apple headquarters and set to work on a product incorporating what he had seen at PARC. In 1983, Apple brought out the Apple Lisa, which was one of the first widely available computers to have GUI. However, the Apple Lisa did not sell well. Most people see its price

INVENTION OF THE MOUSE

Douglas Engelbart, an inventor, engineer, and early computer pioneer, is credited with inventing the computer mouse in the 1960s. He first presented the mouse at a national computer science conference in 1968, though the device did not become common until the late 1980s. His first mouse was made of wood and had metal wheels that moved on the surface it was being used on. Early versions of the mouse had three buttons, though Engelbart thought as many as ten buttons might be useful. Later, when the mouse was added to the Macintosh computer, Jobs decided one button was the best option. Most accounts say it was named a "mouse" because the tail, or cord, came out of the back of the device.

The IBM PC used the already-existing MS–DOS operating system, which meant IBM did not have to write new software for the computer.

tag as one of the major reasons for its failure. At $16,995 for a complete system, it was too expensive for an average PC consumer.[10]

Apple was able to learn from this and improve the Lisa for its next product, the Macintosh, which came out in 1984. The Macintosh introduced the use of icons and GUI to the general public. This changed the whole computing experience from one that could be very technical and intimidating to a more visual and intuitive one. This appealed to people in nontechnical fields, and the Macintosh became a popular tool in education, as well as with artists and designers.

Since 1927, *TIME* magazine has chosen a Person of the Year to appear on the magazine's cover. In 1983, *TIME* named the PC as its Machine of the Year.

Many people consider the Xerox Alto to be the first personal computer.

Microsoft Windows

The introduction of the Macintosh, with its icons and graphics, made the other PCs on the market look old-fashioned. It was clear it was time for the PC to upgrade to a GUI too. Several firms had already started to work on this, but it was technologically difficult and took some time. In 1985, Microsoft came out with Windows 1.0. It drew very heavily from the Macintosh interface in its design, but it did not work as well and it was very slow. In 1987, Windows 2.0 was released. It included expanded memory, as well as desktop icons and better graphics. Three years later, Windows 3.0 was released.

In 1988, Apple filed suit against Microsoft, claiming it had infringed on copyright. Windows 2.0 was essentially identical to the Macintosh interface. Apple feared its unique advantage might be lost. The lawsuit was extremely important for the PC industry. If Apple won, it would likely have a negative effect on all non-Macintosh users. And, developers would believe that all user interfaces would have to be different. As one writer describes,

APPLE'S 1984 COMMERCIAL

Apple launched the Macintosh in a memorable commercial during the Super Bowl in 1984. Drawing from the novel *1984* by George Orwell, it shows a room full of men who look like prisoners watching a huge screen and listening to a figure speak about computers. Everything in the scene is gray and dull. Suddenly, a young woman dressed in bright clothes runs into the room and throws a sledgehammer at the screen. The screen explodes. Then, a message appears, "On January 24, Apple Computer will introduce the Macintosh. And you'll see why 1984 won't be like 1984."[11]

"If Apple were to succeed in the suit, it would be like a car manufacturer being able to copyright the layout of its instruments and every manufacturer having to ensure that its autos had a novel and different instrument layout."[12] The lawsuit went on for three years but was finally dismissed.

Continuing Development

The popularity of PCs continued and, in the coming years, companies brought out new models with faster and more powerful processing capabilities. In 1993, computers began using the Intel Pentium Processor, which significantly improved processing speed and capability.

One of the more notable computer hardware updates was in 1998 when Apple released the iMac. The iMac, an egg-shaped, all-in-one desktop computer, was first offered in bright blue and then came in other bright colors.

From the late 1980s onward, software developers brought out more and more options for software applications. The popularity of IBM PCs and Microsoft Windows encouraged developers to design software for that combination.

During a similar period, computer users began seeing Apple products as tools for desktop publishing and graphic design. The PageMaker desktop publishing application was first released for Apple products in 1985. Two graphic design applications, Adobe Illustrator and Photoshop, were also important because they attracted designers to use the Macintosh instead of PCs.

Consumers loved the iMac alternative to the beige boxes previously offered.

CHAPTER 7

PORTABLE COMPUTERS

OSBORNE 1
User's Reference Guide

Early computers were so heavy the floors often had to be reinforced so the machines would not crash through to the floor below. Now computers can fit in our pockets. As computers began to be viewed as personal devices and cost came down, it was logical people would want to take the machines places. From the 1980s onward, portability became one of the main goals in computer development.

The Osborne I, introduced in 1981, is generally seen as the first portable computer. Compared with today's standards, it was not very portable. However, this was an important invention in the business world, because business people could finally carry both

The Osborne I was approximately the size of a sewing machine, which was considered small in the 1980s.

MODEMS

A modem is a device that allows your computer to access the Internet using telephone or cable lines. The word *modem* is short for "modulator–demodulator." A computer stores data digitally, but information transmitted over phone and cable lines is in analog form. The modem converts between these two forms, so data can be displayed on the computer.

their computer and their computer data with them. The company that made the Osborne I, the Osborne Computer Corporation, never had further success, and it eventually went bankrupt.

The first real laptop, called the GRiD Compass, came out in 1982. It had the now-ubiquitous clamshell design, where a flat display screen folded down onto the keyboard. The GRiD was somewhat successful, but it was very expensive, costing between $8,000 and $10,000.[1] In 1983, two other portable laptops came out—the Compaq Portable and the Epson HX-20. They were more commercially successful. The Compaq was the first portable that was compatible with the MS-DOS operating system. This made it easy to transfer data from a desktop computer to the portable.

The Kyocera Kyotronic was introduced in Japan in 1983. It did not see much success in Japan, but US computer engineers saw its potential and it was more successful in the United States. The Kyotronic weighed less than four pounds (2 kg), had an internal modem, and ran some Microsoft programs. It also cost as little as $300 and had good battery life, so it was especially popular with journalists.[2] The appetite for laptops only increased from there. In 1987, the US Air Force offered a contract for 200,000 laptops, which Zenith Data Systems (ZDS) won. As a result, ZDS was the largest manufacturer of laptops in the late 1980s.

In 1989, Apple finally came out with its own laptop, the Mac Portable, but it was a failure. It was too heavy at 16 pounds (7 kg) and too expensive at $6,500.[3] But Apple came back with the launch of the PowerBook in 1991. It combined the Macintosh operating system with the innovation of a trackball or trackpad in front of the keyboard so users could rest their wrists and use the computer on their laps. The IBM ThinkPad, which came out in 1992, had a sleek, elegant styling.

The release of Windows 95 by Microsoft in 1995 was a milestone because it standardized many aspects of laptop design. Before that, operating systems for laptops varied. Intel also came out with its Pentium processor, and CD-ROM drives became standard on laptops. All of this took

The Compass was the first laptop, but it was expensive, which limited its market.

THE DYNABOOK

Back in the 1960s, it would have been difficult to imagine how small computers would become, but a few people did. In 1968, computer scientist Alan Kay, who was a pioneer in GUI design, came up with the concept of a thin, portable computer. He called it the "dynamic book," or Dynabook, and it would be aimed particularly at children. The computer was never built because it was too far ahead of technology at the time. Kay and others continued developing the concept, and his work is seen as highly influential in the field. Most of the features of his Dynabook, including wireless capability, have now been incorporated into tablet computers.

the laptop from its bulky, heavy beginnings to the relatively lightweight models we know today.

Handhelds

Early electronic handheld calculators were the predecessors to handheld devices such as smartphones that we use today. The Busicom Handy LE-120A was one of the first electronic calculators that fit into a pocket. It included functions for later handheld devices: processor, display, keys, battery, and memory. The handhelds that focused on a specific function, such as a calendar, address book, or cookbook, were most successful in the early days.

Many people do not realize the first personal digital assistant (PDA) was the Psion Organiser, which came out in 1984. The Psion looked similar to a calculator, but it was actually a computer. In 1986, the Psion Organiser II was released with many improvements. As a result, Psion sold more than 1 million devices in its line of handhelds.[4]

The Palm Pilot was a general-purpose computer that could track contacts, notes, to-do lists, and events. It also synchronized all of this data to a desktop computer. A major reason for the Palm Pilot's success was that it established the handheld as an accessory to a PC, not as a replacement. It also helped that the price of $299 was reasonable.[5]

Early Smartphones

BellSouth and IBM introduced the first smartphone in 1992, although it did not go on sale until 1994. It was called Simon, and it was not actually labeled a *smartphone* because the term was not yet in use. The phone weighed more than one pound (0.5 kg) and cost more than $800.[6] It did not have a web browser, but users could access e-mail and send faxes. Simon is believed to be the first commercially available phone with a touch screen. A stylus was included to navigate the screen, or people could use their finger. Cell phones were not yet widely in use, and service was not always easy to find in the early 1990s, but Simon could also be plugged into a phone jack. Simon was not very successful. Approximately 50,000 phones were sold and it was on the market for only six months.[7]

THE APPLE NEWTON

The Apple Newton tablet, which was released in 1993, is generally considered a failure. The aim was to create a tablet to replace a desktop computer, for a similar price, and to open up a new market. A major feature of the Newton was handwriting recognition, but a big problem was that it was not actually good at recognizing handwriting. Although it was not successful, many people believe it still affected the industry.

Art Institute of Chicago

in Chicago, Ill., museum of European, American, and Oriental sculpture, paintings, prints and drawings, and decorative arts, as well as photography and African and pre-Columbian American art. It was established in 1866 as the Chicago Academy of Design and took its current name in 1882. In 1893 it moved to its present building.

britannica.com

Fine Institute...

History

In 1996, Nokia released the Nokia 9000 Communicator, which was capable of e-mail, fax, web browsing, word processing, and even working with spreadsheets. The phone's design was notable because it looked like a cell phone from the outside, but it had a hinge that opened up to a full QWERTY keyboard. This phone was also a smartphone, but still was not called one.

The first all-in-one device to be called a smartphone was launched in 2000 by Ericsson. Smartphones really took off and became popular in the early 2000s. New capabilities and features such as cameras, MP3 players, and wireless technology made the devices more and more popular with consumers. Between 2000 and 2006, cell phone manufacturers explored different designs to increase functionality and ease of use. Some phones featured flip keyboards, whereas others used sliding keyboards or other designs. The stylus came into use as touchscreens were incorporated into smartphone design.

iPhone and Android

In 2007, the Apple iPhone was released, which dramatically changed the smartphone world. Many iPhone features have now become standard on almost all phones made. One example is the screen. Before the iPhone came out, most phones had keyboards

The first mobile telephone call was placed in 1946. This eventually led to wireless telephone networks that we use today.

The Palm Pilot was the first successful handheld computer.

Smartphones quickly changed in the 2000s as manufacturers created more functional designs.

that took approximately one-third of the front side of the phone. The interface between the screen and the user has changed as well. The multitouch controls on the iPhone revolutionized how we manipulate the screen. Then there was the price: when the iPhone 3G came out in 2008, it was $199 compared with $400 or more for other phones.[8] Finally, the iPhone popularized apps by offering the App Store and making it easy to browse, buy, and install apps.

The introduction of the iPhone radically changed the smartphone landscape, but competition soon appeared. In 2008, Internet search company Google released its Android operating system. It is a free operating system. Google's strategy in making it free was to give it away to make it the dominant operating system to compete against Apple and the iPhone. The strategy worked. Other smartphone manufacturers were desperate to come up with competition against the iPhone, so they were willing to use the Android operating system. Android was also quickly available on all of the

Only four years after it was released, the iPhone made up 39 percent of Apple's overall revenue.[9]

Apple iPhones continue to be powerful and efficient smartphones.

WHAT IS AN APP?

The word *app* is short for "application," so an app is a type of software. It can run on the Internet, on a computer, or on a smartphone or other mobile device. The word *app*, which really refers to a program, came into common use because of the popularity of mobile devices. In 2010, the American Dialect Society voted the word *app* as its word of the year.

major phone carriers, but Apple was available with only one provider for a long time.

The Tablet Computer

The history of the tablet computer goes back further than people might realize. And the roots of the tablet are in both handheld devices and laptops. The Linus Write-Top was a handwriting-recognition tablet that came out in 1987. A user could write with a stylus on a green screen. That was followed in 1989 by the GridPad tablet, which is often called the first tablet computer. The GridPad weighed 4.5 pounds (2 kg) and cost more than $2,000.[10] It did not sell well, possibly because of its cost and weight compared with laptops at the time.

In 2000, Bill Gates introduced a prototype for a tablet computer. Some people credit Microsoft for introducing the term *tablet*. By the mid-2000s, several tablet computers were on the market. However, they were still expensive and not very popular with the average consumer. It was not until 2010, when the iPad was

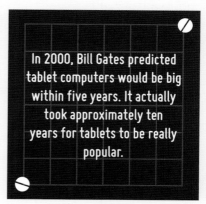

In 2000, Bill Gates predicted tablet computers would be big within five years. It actually took approximately ten years for tablets to be really popular.

released, that tablets really took off. Consumers had already grown to appreciate the touch screen of Apple products, and that helped its popularity. Some people predicted the iPad would fail, but it did not. Instead, it has surpassed all expectations.

Following the success of the iPad, competitors jumped in. Tablets running the Android operating system soon arrived, including the Samsung Galaxy Tab. Because of its high price, it was not successful right away. When the price finally dropped, it became more attractive to buyers. The open-source Android operating system eventually created more variety in the market at lower prices. Since then, other tablets have arrived. Amazon's Kindle Fire was launched in 2011 at a price of $199.[11] This was significant because it showed a tablet with reasonable quality could be affordable.

SMARTPHONE USES

When most people think of smartphones, they think of a device to entertain, socialize, and keep up with work. But some surprising uses have been found for smartphones. Researchers have found that sensors in Android phones that measure battery temperature, light, and pressure can also be used to create fairly accurate weather reports. Another use is an app that turns a smartphone into a mobile medical lab. It uses the phone's camera to detect toxins, viruses, and other organisms.

The Internet

The Internet is the global system of interconnected computer networks that links several billion devices worldwide. It has become such an integral part of all our lives that it can be easy to forget that it is relatively new. Early on, as software became standardized, it became clear, especially in the business world, that linking computers in a network was useful for sharing information. Initially, computers were linked in local area networks, but then people wanted to link computers over larger distances. In the 1960s and 1970s, the US Department of Defense developed a network called ARPANET, which is generally considered to be a predecessor to the Internet. Other networks were created later, and in the late 1980s, these networks came together to create what we now call the Internet. In 1989, software engineer Tim Berners-Lee invented the virtual network of websites that is called the World Wide Web. The original purpose of both the Internet and the World Wide Web was related to searching for and exchanging information. Today, the Internet is a tool that allows users to access information and communicate with people in constantly changing and evolving ways.

The Internet is easily accessible through the countless number of machines available today, including tablets.

CHAPTER 8

THE FUTURE OF
COMPUTING

Computer experts are always looking ahead and trying to predict what computing of the future might look like. Of course, no one can be sure exactly what technologies will emerge. However, there is always plenty of speculation, and there are areas of research most experts believe will produce results in the not-too-distant future.

Nanotechnology

Nanotechnology is an important area of research and development for computing technologies, as well as many other applications. Nanotechnology is science, technology, and engineering carried

Computer technology, including 3-D printers, will continue to grow as research expands.

Gold and silver particles used to create the colors in stained glass windows in medieval churches are examples of nanoscale materials.

out at the nanoscale, which is approximately 1 to 100 nanometers. To show how small nanoscale is, consider that approximately 25,400,000 nanometers are in 1 inch (2.5 cm). A sheet of newspaper is approximately 100,000 nanometers thick.[1]

Nanotechnology is already being used in many commercial products and processes. It is used to manufacture products that need to be both lightweight and strong, such as sporting equipment and auto parts. It is also being used in many situations to save energy and reduce waste. Almost any high-performance electronic device that was built in the past decade incorporates some nanomaterial. Nanotechnology is also being used in medicine, and scientists believe there will soon be even more helpful and exciting applications for medicine. For example, nanotechnology can be used to make imaging like MRI and CAT scans more safe and effective. Nanotechnology will soon help deliver medicine in a safer way by using nanoparticles in medicine to target tumors directly and reduce drug damage to other parts of the body.

A Wonder Material

An example of a new material in nanotechnology is graphene. In 2010, two physicists, Konstantin Novoselov and Andre Geim, shared the Nobel Prize for their work developing a new material that could possibly revolutionize electronics in

Hewlett Packard technicians work on nanotechnology research to create different types of computer chips.

Andre Geim, *left*, and Dr. Konstantin Novoselov, *right*, predict graphene could replace silicon in transistors at some point in the future.

the future. Graphene, is a flat carbon material that is only one atom thick. It is transparent, highly conductive, and is the strongest material known to science. Novoselov and Geim discovered the material by putting sticky tape onto graphite.

GOOGLE'S SELF-DRIVING CAR

Launched in 2009, the Google Self-Driving Car project develops technology for electric cars that transfers control from the human driver to a computer. One day, this technology may allow drivers to be hands-free during their commutes. The cars have a laser range finder mounted on the roof of the car. This laser creates 3-D maps, which are combined with high-resolution maps of the world. These maps help the computer avoid obstacles and follow traffic laws. The car also has radar, a camera, and a GPS system. All self-driving cars must also have a human operating the vehicle in case of emergencies.

Google employees are currently testing Google's computer system, Google Chauffeur, in a variety of cars. The cars have logged more than 700,000 miles (1.1 million km) without any accidents.[4] However, the latest prototype in 2014 was unable to drive in heavy rain or in snowy conditions. Google hopes to have the computer system completed and any adjustments refined in the next ten years.

Novoselov believes that graphene has great potential for the electronics industry. Transistors will likely get smaller and smaller, so scientists will be looking for alternatives to current materials and technologies. However, his view is that graphene will not just be another alternative material, but that it could be part of a "completely new architecture."[2] He hopes, "Within a few layers of atoms we will be able to encode the logic circuit, the power unit and so on. You would have a flexible, transparent or semitransparent, multifunctional material that has functions encoded into its structure."[3]

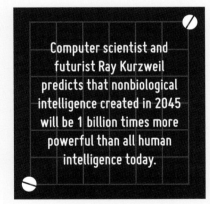

Computer scientist and futurist Ray Kurzweil predicts that nonbiological intelligence created in 2045 will be 1 billion times more powerful than all human intelligence today.

PASSING THE
TURING TEST

I n 1950, Alan Turing introduced the idea of a test to see if a computer could pass as a human, called the Turing Test. In 2011, IBM's Watson computer system competed on the game show *Jeopardy!* against two former winners. Watson went on to win the game. The computer's storage was full of millions of pages of content, but the machine was not connected to the Internet during the game. To answer a question, Watson displayed its top three answers on its screen. Since winning *Jeopardy!*, Watson systems are being used in the health-care industry with IBM wanting to further expansion.

In 2014, it was reported that a chatbot, which is a computer program designed to simulate human conversation, had tricked judges into believing it was human. This chatbot was supposed to be a 13-year-old boy named Eugene Goostman living in Ukraine. There is a lot of disagreement about whether this was an accurate Turing Test. Some experts say the test was too simple and also too short, so therefore do not accept the results. However, whether it was accurate or not, many experts agree the debate shows artificial intelligence is moving closer to a point where a computer might actually pass a Turing Test.

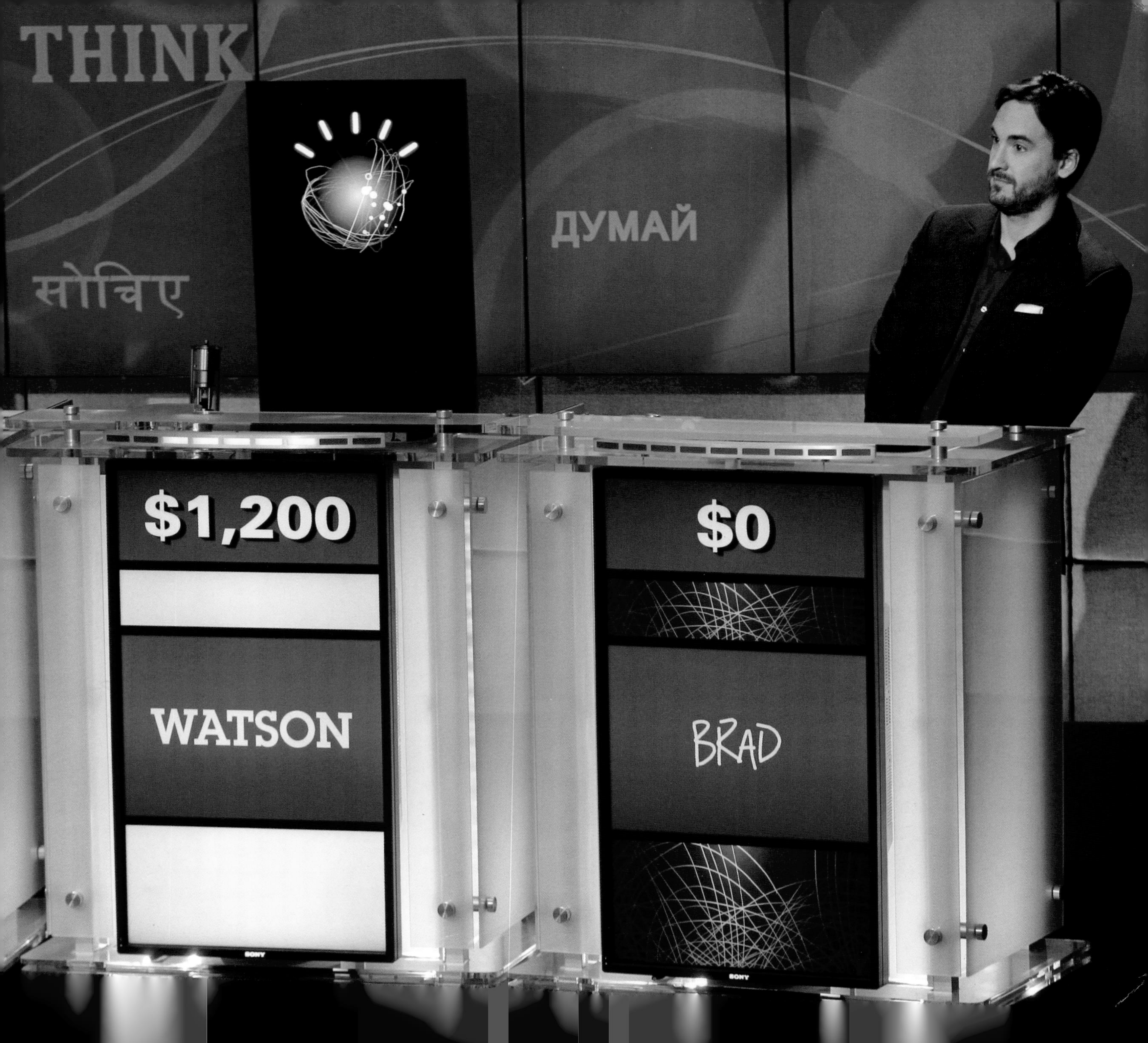
THINK
सोचिए
ДУМАЙ
$1,200
WATSON
$0
BRAD
SONY
SONY

Artificial Intelligence

Artificial intelligence (AI) is a field of study that works to give computers humanlike qualities. Many advances have already been made in the field of AI, including speech recognition and navigation. Most experts believe advances will be made very quickly in the coming decades. Scientists and engineers are working on self-driving cars, robots that can do everything from factory work to emergency rescues, and machines that can recognize people and "understand" their emotions.

However, there is debate whether advances in artificial intelligence could create risks for humans. Some scientists fear it could be bad for humans as artificial intelligence is developed without safety precautions. The concept of the point when artificial intelligence becomes smarter than humans is called "technological singularity." It is a topic of intense discussion among experts because no knows or can really extrapolate what would happen after the singularity point. Scientist Stephen Hawking said in an interview, "Once humans develop artificial intelligence, it will take off on its own and redesign itself at an ever-increasing rate. Humans, who are limited by slow biological evolution, couldn't compete and would be superseded."[5]

Supercomputing

A supercomputer is a computer, or a network of computers, that is among the fastest and most powerful in the world. Supercomputers can process huge sets of data and help scientists solve complex equations that reflect real-life problems and questions. Supercomputers are used to predict weather patterns and climate change, test and study nuclear weapons, and model aspects of the human body such as the flow of blood.

The main goal for the future of supercomputing is increasing the speed and power of the computers. In 2014, researchers said machines with significantly better speed and efficiency could be released within one year.

THE SEQUOIA AND TITAN SUPERCOMPUTERS

The Sequoia and the Titan are two of the biggest and fastest supercomputers. The Sequoia, which is at the Lawrence Livermore National Laboratory in Livermore, California, was named the fastest supercomputer in 2012. In one hour, the Sequoia can calculate what it would take 6.7 billion people using hand calculators and working 24 hours per day 320 years to do.[6] Only six months later, the Titan, which is at the US Department of Energy's Oak Ridge Lab in Tennessee, replaced the Sequoia as the fastest supercomputer. The Titan is as large as a basketball court and uses as much power as it takes to run a small town. Researchers use the Titan to study climate change, alternative fuels, and nuclear power simulation.

Computers of all types have transformed virtually every aspect of human life in a very short span of time. These devices have changed the way people interact with family, friends, and their surroundings. Not only has all of this development happened in a short time frame, but also the rate of change continues increasing rapidly. It seems likely developments and innovation will continue, perhaps at an even faster rate than ever before.

In 2008, Stan Williams, the founder of Hewlett-Packard's elite research lab HP Labs, gave some of his opinions about the future of computers and technology. He said then, "The age of computing has not yet begun. What we have now makes the computers that existed 50 years ago look like toys—and not very good ones. My view is that what we'll have in 50 years will make what we have now look very quaint and toylike."[7]

IBM released its robot Pepper in 2014 in Tokyo, Japan. Pepper is "engaging and emotionally intelligent," according to IBM.

THE NEXT
GENERATION: WEARABLE COMPUTERS

Many experts see wearable computers, or computers that are worn on the body or incorporated into clothing, as the latest breakthrough in computing. There is a wide range of wearable products already on the market, or very near to being on the market. Types of products include glasses, watches, contact lenses, jewelry, wristbands, and "smart" fabrics and clothing. One of the most popular early uses of wearable computers is for health and fitness. Users wear a wristband, watch, or other device, and the wearable computer monitors the user's sleep patterns, exercise, heart rate, and more. More of these kinds of devices are being incorporated into clothing.

Health-care companies are also working to apply these innovations to specific medical conditions. For example, wearable devices monitor insulin levels for diabetics. Pills with a computer

Google Glass

Fitbit

Smart watch

chip for monitoring a patient's health are another example.

Google Glass is one of the most well known types of smart glasses, but experts predict more will be forthcoming. Features of this type of glasses might include cameras, compass, Wi-Fi, and Bluetooth. One variation of Google Glass is a set of ski goggles with a display that shows information on speed and distance, as well as text messages and ski resort maps.

A general trend in wearable computers is making them look stylish. Whether it is a watch, a piece of jewelry, or an item of clothing, companies are designing them with style and fashion in mind.

ESSENTIAL FACTS

DATE OF INVENTION

1947: The transistor is invented.

1958: The integrated circuit is invented.

1971: The microprocessor is invented.

1993: The first smartphone is introduced.

KEY PLAYERS

▶ William Shockley, John Bardeen, and Walter Brattain, coinventors of the transistor

▶ Jack Kilby and Robert Noyce, coinventors of the integrated circuit

▶ Bill Gates, cofounder with Paul Allen, of Microsoft

▶ Steve Jobs, cofounder with Steve Wozniak, of Apple

KEY TECHNOLOGIES

▶ The transistor

▶ The integrated circuit

▶ The microprocessor

▶ The personal computer

▶ The smartphone

EVOLUTION AND UPGRADES

Since early on, visionaries have driven the development of computers. Those inventors, engineers, and entrepreneurs constantly looked for ways to improve the machine. They started with mechanical, analog machines, and progressed to electronic, digital computers. The goal has always been to make computers smaller and faster, yet as powerful and efficient, as they can be. There may be differing views as to exactly what technologies will emerge in the future, but those goals will likely remain the same.

IMPACT ON SOCIETY

Computer technology has affected virtually every aspect of human experience. Everyday activities from shopping to socializing rely on computer technology to make those processes easier and more efficient. Larger societal interests from government, to medicine, to space exploration also depend on computer technology. In particular, communication has been radically transformed as the result of recent advances in technology.

QUOTE

"The age of computing has not yet begun. What we have now makes the computers that existed 50 years ago look like toys—and not very good ones. My view is that what we'll have in 50 years will make what we have now look very quaint and toylike."

—*Stan Williams, founder of HP Labs*

GLOSSARY

application

A computer program, or piece of software, designed to enable the user to carry out a function.

binary

A numbering system that uses the two values of 0 and 1 for each digit.

bit

Short for "binary digit," which is the smallest unit of information on a computer.

Bluetooth

A computing and telecommunications specification that describes how mobile phones, computers, and other devices can easily connect with one another using a short-range wireless connection.

circuit

The complete path that an electric current passes along.

conductor

A substance that allows electricity, heat, or sound to pass through it.

digital

Using numbers (usually binary) to process, store, and show a computer's calculations.

hardware

The fixed and solid parts of a computer (for example, the monitor and display).

insulator

A material that is a poor conductor of electricity.

logarithm

The power to which a base such as 10 must be raised to produce a given number.

open-source

Software having the original source code made freely available for redistribution and modification.

operating system

Software that lets the computer perform basic functions.

patent

A permit issued by a government that grants a person the legal right to use or market an invention, technology, or process.

seismology

The science that deals with earthquakes and vibration of the earth.

semiconductor

Any of a set of materials that conduct electricity between a conductor and an insulator.

software

A set of instructions that tells a computer to perform a certain task.

solder

A metal or mix of metals used to join metallic surfaces.

Wi-Fi

A technology that enables connection to the Internet by radio waves, without added wires or cables, by creating a small Wi-Fi network within a building, such as a home, café, or airport.

wireless

Using radio, microwaves, etc. (instead of wires or cables) to transmit signals.

SELECTED BIBLIOGRAPHY

Campbell-Kelly, Martin. *Computer: A History of the Information Machine*. New York: Basic, 1996. Print.

Ceruzzi, Paul E. *A History of Modern Computing*. London: MIT, 2003. Print.

Chaline, Eric. *Fifty Machines That Changed the Course of History*. Buffalo, NY: Firefly, 2012. Print.

Reid, T. R. *The Chip: How Two Americans Invented the Microchip and Launched a Revolution*. New York: Simon, 1984. Print.

"Timeline of Computer History." *Computer History Museum*. Computer History Museum, 2006. Web. 13 Mar. 2015.

FURTHER READINGS

Campbell-Kelly, Martin. *Computer: A History of the Information Machine*. Boulder, CO: Westview, 2014. Print.

Farrell, Mary. *Computer Programming for Teens*. Boston: Thomson Course Technology PTR, 2008. Print.

Sande, Warren. *Hello World!: Computer Programming for Kids and Other Beginners*. Greenwich, CT: Manning, 2009. Print.

Woodford, Chris. *Communication and Computers*. New York: Facts on File, 2004. Print.

WEBSITES

To learn more about Essential Library of Inventions, visit **booklinks.abdopublishing.com**. These links are routinely monitored and updated to provide the most current information available.

FOR MORE INFORMATION

For more information on this subject, contact or visit the following organizations:

Association for Information Science and Technology

8555 16th Street, Suite 850
Silver Spring, Maryland 20910
301-495-0900
http://www.asist.org

The Association for Information Science and Technology is a group for information professionals, allowing them to access techniques and technologies.

Computer History Museum

1401 North Shoreline Boulevard
Mountain View, CA 94043
650-810-1010
http://www.computerhistory.org

The Computer History Museum is the world's largest museum containing stories and artifacts from the Information Age. The museum is located in Silicon Valley, California.

The IEEE Computer Society

2001 L Street NW, Suite 700
Washington, DC 20036
202-371-0101
http://www.computer.org

The IEEE Computer Society is a global organization of computer professionals. They work to further technology.

SOURCE NOTES

Chapter 1. The Interconnections Problem

1. T. R. Reid. *The Chip: How Two Americans Invented the Microchip and Launched a Revolution*. New York: Simon, 1984. Print. 17–19.

2. Ibid.

3. "About Jack." *Texas Instruments*. Texas Instruments Incorporated, 2015. Web. 25 Mar. 2015.

4. "Robert Noyce." *PBS*. ScienCentral, Inc., 1999. Web. 25 Mar. 2015.

5. Martin Campbell-Kelly. *Computer: A History of the Information Machine*. New York: Basic, 1996. Print. 3.

Chapter 2. Early History

1. Victor Kotsev. "The First Computers, Lasers, Robots, and More: Ancient Innovations From Our Distant Ancestors." *Fast Company*. Mansueto Ventures, 18 Feb. 2014. Web. 25 Mar. 2015.

2. "Schickard's Calculator and the Pascaline." *Computer History Museum*. Computer History Museum, 2015. Web. 25 Mar. 2015.

3. Michael R. Swaine. "Difference Engine." *Encyclopedia Britannica*. Encyclopedia Britannica, 12 Aug. 2013. Web. 25 Mar. 2015.

4. Doron Swade. "The Babbage Engine." *Computer History Museum*. Computer History Museum, 2008. Web. 25 Mar. 2015.

5. Georges Ifrah. *The Universal History of Computing: From the Abacus to the Quantum Computer*. New York: John Wiley, 2001. Print. 191.

Chapter 3. From People to Machines

1. Martin Campbell-Kelly. *Computer: A History of the Information Machine*. New York: Basic, 1996. Print. 20–21.

2. "Making Sense of the Census: Hollerith's Punched Card Solution." *Computer History Museum*. Computer History Museum, 2015. Web. 25 Mar. 2015.

3. Vannevar Bush. "As We May Think." *Atlantic*. Atlantic Monthly Group, 1 July 1945. Web. 25 Mar. 2015.

4. Martin Campbell-Kelly. *Computer: A History of the Information Machine*. New York: Basic, 1996. Print. 70–76.

5. Ibid. 72–74.

6. B. Jack Copeland, and Diane Proudfoot. "Alan Turing: Father of the Modern Computer." *Rutherford Journal*. RutherfordJournal.org, 2012. Web. 25 Mar. 2015.

7. Martin Campbell-Kelly. *Computer: A History of the Information Machine*. New York: Basic, 1996. Print. 72–74.

Chapter 4. Calculating Machines

1. "ENIAC." *Computer History Museum*. Computer History Museum, 2015. Web. 25 Mar. 2015.

2. "ENIAC." *Computer History Museum*. Computer History Museum, 2015. Web. 25 Mar. 2015.

3. Jan Van der Spiegel. "ENIAC-on-a-Chip." *Moore School of Electrical Engineering*. University of Pennsylvania, 27 Dec. 2012. Web. 25 Mar. 2015.

4. "The Stored Program." *Computer History Museum*. Computer History Museum, 2015. Web. 25 Mar. 2015.

5. "UNIVAC." *Computer History Museum*. Computer History Museum, 2015. Web. 25 Mar. 2015.

6. Martin Campbell-Kelly. *Computer: A History of the Information Machine*. New York: Basic, 1996. Print. 121–123.

Chapter 5. The Second Generation

1. "The First Transistorized Computer." *PBS*. ScienCentral, Inc., 1999. Web. 25 Mar. 2015.

2. "Fairchild Semiconductor." *PBS*. ScienCentral, Inc., 1999. Web. 25 Mar. 2015.

3. Michael Aaron Dennis. "Silicon Valley." *Encyclopedia Britannica*. Encyclopedia Britannica, 13 Jan. 2015. Web. 25 Mar. 2015.

4. Steven J. Vaughan-Nichols. "Ten Years of IBM Mainframe Linux." *ComputerWorld*. ComputerWorld, 8 June 2010. Web. 25 Mar. 2015.

5. Gordon Bell. "Rise and Fall of Minicomputers." *Engineering and Technology History Wiki*. ETHW, 9 Jan. 2015. Web. 25 Mar. 2015.

6. "Smaller is Better." *Computer History Museum*. Computer History Museum, 2015. Web. 25 Mar. 2015.

7. "Bytes for Bites: The Kitchen Computer." *Computer History Museum*. Computer History Museum, 2015. Web. 25 Mar. 2015.

Chapter 6. One Chip

1. Paul E. Ceruzzi. *A History of Modern Computing*. London: MIT, 2003. Print. 218–221.

2. Martin Campbell-Kelly. *Computer: A History of the Information Machine*. New York: Basic, 1996. Print. 237.

3. "The *Altair 8800* of Ed Roberts." *History of Computers*. Georgi Dalakov, 2015. Web. 27 Apr. 2015.

4. Alice Kreit and Jessica Wanke. "Timeline: Bill Gates." *NPR*. National Public Radio, 2015. Web. 25 Mar. 2015.

5. "The Homebrew Computer Club." *Computer History Museum*. Computer History Museum, 2015. Web. 25 Mar. 2015.

6. Martin Campbell-Kelly. *Computer: A History of the Information Machine*. New York: Basic, 1996. Print. 246.

7. Ibid. 248.

8. Richard Fletcher. "PC World Announces the End of the Floppy Disk." *Telegraph*. Telegraph Media Group, 30 Jan. 2007. Web. 27 Apr. 2015.

9. Martin Campbell-Kelly. *Computer: A History of the Information Machine*. New York: Basic, 1996. Print. 270.

10. Ibid. 271.

11. Ibid. 274.

12. Ibid. 279.

13. "Linux." *Computer History Museum*. Computer History Museum, 2015. Web. 25 Mar. 2015.

Chapter 7. Portable Computers

1. "The History of the Laptop Computer." *Random History*. RandomHistory.com, 5 May 2007. Web. 25 Mar. 2015.

2. Ibid.

3. "Laptops Emerge." *Computer History Museum*. Computer History Museum, 2015. Web. 25 Mar. 2015.

4. "Handhelds and Tablets." *Computer History Museum*. Computer History Museum, 2015. Web. 25 Mar. 2015.

5. "The PalmPilot." *Computer History Museum*. Computer History Museum, 2015. Web. 25 Mar. 2015.

6. Doug Aamoth. "First Smartphone Turns 20: Fun Facts About Simon." *TIME*. TIME, 18 Aug. 2014. Web. 25 Mar. 2015.

7. Ibid.

8. Dan Frommer. "History Lesson: How the iPhone Changed Smartphones Forever." *Business Insider*. Business Insider, 6 June 2011. Web. 25 Mar. 2015.

9. Henry Blodget. "15 Amazing Facts about Apple." *Business Insider*. Business Insider, 28 Oct. 2010. Web. 25 Mar. 2015.

10. "GRiDPad." *OldComputers.net*. OldComputers.net, 10 Dec. 2013. Web. 25 Mar. 2015.

11. Julie Bort. "The History of the Tablet, An Idea Steve Jobs Stole and Turned Into a Game-Changer." *Business Insider*. Business Insider, 2 June 2013. Web. 25 Mar. 2015.

Chapter 8. The Future of Computing

1. "What is Nanotechnology?" *Nano.gov*. United States National Nanotechnology Initiative, 2015. Web. 25 Mar. 2015.

2. Katia Moskvitch. "A Graphene Discoverer Speculates on the Future of Computing." *Scientific American*. Scientific American, 23 Jan. 2015. Web. 25 Mar. 2015.

3. Ibid.

4. Chris Urmson. "The Latest Chapter for the Self-Driving Car: Mastering City Street Driving." *Google*. Google, 28 Apr. 2014. Web. 25 Mar. 2015.

5. Dominic Basulto. "Why the World's Most Intelligent People Shouldn't Be So Afraid of Artificial Intelligence." *Washington Post*. Washington Post, 20 Jan. 2015. Web. 25 Mar. 2015.

6. "Sustainable Stockpile Stewardship." *Advanced Simulation and Computing*. Lawrence Livermore National Security, 1 Oct. 2012. Web. 25 Mar. 2015.

7. Wendy M. Grossman. "HP Machine: Memristor Pioneer Explains His Discovery." *Inquirer*. Incisive Business Media, 17 June 2014. Web. 25 Mar 2015.

INDEX

About the Author

Therese Naber is a writer who lives in Minnesota. She has coauthored more than ten textbooks and workbooks for students and teachers of English as a Second Language. She has also written many tests and online activities for language learning. This is her third nonfiction book for young people.

Keyboard

Mouse

Input: taking in data

Hard drive

Memory: storing information

Central processing unit (CPU): processes information

Microchip

Output: information that comes out

Monitor

Printer

CHAPTER 6

ONE
CHIP

The next major innovation in computer history arrived in 1971: the microprocessor. Similar to other developments in the history of the computer, there was more than one person working on a similar invention around the same time. However, Ted Hoff, an engineer at Intel Corporation, is generally credited with the invention of the microprocessor.

Intel was started in 1968 in Santa Clara, California, and specialized in making custom-designed chips that were used in items such as calculators, video games, and equipment for electronic testing. In 1969, a Japanese company that sold handheld